between
Zen
and
Tao

M Scotty Cogdell

between Zen and Tao
M Scotty Cogdell

ISBN 13: 978-0615655703
ISBN 10: 061565570x

mr. ma'at publishing

This book is dedicated to everyone that has ever stubbed a toe or two walking barefoot along the spiritual path.

Disclaimer:
The author assumes no responsibility if the reader has uncontrollable fits of laughter, genuine smiles, head shaking, or a sense of well being as a result of reading this book.

Table of Contents:

1. Aum, Nothing

The search for nothing. Science, both modern and ancient, make the attempt to discover and explain the existence of everything. The threshold of this discovery is within the search of nothing. An example of this is the search for the Higgs-Bosom Particle, or the search for the Atman. Another example is Einstein's Theory of Relativity, or the concept of Yin and Yang. Take the String Theory, for example, which basically states that everything in the known universe is connected. This is considered a cutting edge, ultra-modern modality of thinking. What is overlooked is that this is the modality of being for so-called "primitive" peoples' existence. Science is attempting to explain the singularity of nothing. Spirituality reveals nothingness, which cannot be explained. As Lao Tzu has stated,
"the Tao that can be spoken of is not the Tao." Guatam the Buddha teaches that nothing is real and everything is a projection of the mind.

Enlightenment is yours already. You can't run away from it, and no one can keep it from you. It can't be bought, sold, or even given away. Most people won't recognize it when they see it, yet most wonder how it can be attained. The secret, if told, would no longer be a secret. Where might spiritual enlightenment be found? Maybe somewhere between Zen and Tao...

2. The Tao of Yogurt

It will slim you down, keep you in shape, and it's good for you. That's what most people say about yogurt. That's also what most people say about Yoga. Yet Yoga is much more than this. When most people think of Yoga, it is the numerous stretches and postures (asanas) of Hatha Yoga that come to mind. My teacher (a Yogi trained in India) calls this ideology "Hollywood" Yoga-- using Yoga as only a simple physical exercise. There is much more to Yoga than just the postures (asanas). The meaning of the word Yoga is "to yoke," or "union with God."

There are eight precepts or "limbs" of Yoga as described by the Indian sage Pantanjali. All of these must be in place to truly practice Yoga. This discourse is not meant to be a discussion of the classic view of Yoga in a strict sense, but a perspective of Yogic principles from a contemporary point of view.

Following is a brief outline of the eight limbs of Yoga, each explained further in depth as we continue along this journey.

The Eight Limbs of Yoga:

    I. Yama: Restraints
   II. Niyama: Observances
  III. Asana: Posture(s)
  IV. Pranayam: Breath (control/regulation of)
   V. Pratyahara: Involution
  VI. Dharana: Concentration
 VII. Dhyana: Meditation
VIII. Samadhi: Bliss

I. Yama (Restraints)

As with anything, there are certain things not to do if one wishes
to do something. For example, when cleaning up, don't mix
bleach and ammonia--that is a practical restraint. In the
discipline of Yoga, there are five restraints, or Yamas.
    1. Ahimsa: non-violence
    2. Satya: truthfulness
    3. Asteya: non-stealing
    4. Bramacharya: sexual discipline
    5. Aparigraha: non-possessiveness

1. Ahimsa: non- violence

Anybody familiar with the Ten Commandments? Thou Shalt Not Kill? This is the same concept, applied to ALL life, from mouse to man. One thing must be realized, though. It is impossible to achieve, for even in the very act of breathing millions of micro-organisms are killed. To paraphrase Swami Sri Yukteswarji, practical application of Ahimsa isn't not killing, but not having the intent of committing violence. If it is one's duty as a soldier, in self protection, or protecting others (such as children from a venomous snake), no bad karma ensues from not strictly adhering to the concept of Ahimsa. This is clearly explained by Krishna to Arjuna in the Baghavad Gita, when Arjuna, as a warrior, was reluctant to go to battle. Krishna informed Arjuna that not fulfilling his prescribed duty (of vanquishing his opponents) would be sinful. What's my view of Ahimsa? Turn the other cheek, just remember to duck.

2. Satya: truthfulness

Basically, "Thou Shalt Not Lie." I would like to add "Thou Shalt Not Lie, Especially To Yourself!" It's one thing to lie to others, because you blatantly recognize the lie. Lying to oneself, on the other hand, may be perpetuated to one's own detriment infinitely, because either the lie isn't recognized as a lie, or the ego justifies it. This is one of the biggest impediments to spiritual growth, because dishonesty doesn't allow you to see things as they really are. If you don't like your reality, then change it. If you can't change it, then accept the fact that things are the way they are. Get on with living life, instead of wasting energy 'trying to blow the Sun out,' because you want it to be nighttime. The Serenity Prayer hit the nail on the head with this one.

The Serenity Prayer:

God, grant me the strength to change the things I can,
Serenity to accept the things I can't,
And Wisdom to know the difference.

3. Asteya: non-stealing

This one should be fairly self-explanatory. Thou Shalt Not Steal. Are you starting to notice some similarities between two supposedly different ways of life? If you need something, ask. If not, Get Your Hand Out My Pocket!

4. Bramacharya: sexual discipline

Traditionally, this meant celibacy. I personally prefer a Tantric lifestyle. Don't make love with someone you're not in love with. Sexual energy is the most powerful energy known to humankind. Learn how to use it properly, and don't abuse it. Here's a poem by me on my application of this Yama (Bramacharya):

Maybe:

being celibate
is my medicine
for loneliness
like water still
i enjoy
the physical pleasures
of having a relationship
but only with
one who makes
my mind content
whom with
long strolls
through the gardens of life
in which our souls
will be holding hands
hearing each others' voice
listening to every word
finding our way
by getting lost
in conversation

5. Aparigraha: non-possessiveness

Don't be selfish. Share what you can. Everything we have that's material we will have to eventually leave behind, anyway. If you have something you don't need, or are not using, why not help somebody out, or contribute to another's happiness? For example, if you have a hammer you are not using, or even picked up in years, and your neighbor needs to use it for work, or to build a child's toybox (or anything else), let her/him use it. Don't be like a toddler: "MINE!" For those of you with children, you know what usually happens next. The same applies to you (yes, you!). The Universe is impartial to the rich and poor alike, and will spank that ass. Remember, sharing is caring.

II. Niyama (Observances)

There is a saying in the world of martial arts that "to be without a method is unforgivable." Anyone with parents (that should be everyone) can remember the statement, "wash your hands before you eat." An observance those of us who drive a stick keeps is to press the clutch in to start the car/motorcycle, or to change gears. A simple observance everybody keeps (I hope everybody keeps) is to wipe your ass after you take a shit. Yes, Yoga has its observances also. There are five Niyamas, or observances for the practice of Yoga.

1. Shaucha: purity
2. Santosha: contentment
3. Tapas: austerity
4. Swadihyaya: introspection
5. Ishwarapranidhana: devotion to God

1. Shaucha: purity

In the practical sense, keep everything clean as you can. Your home, car, clothes, body, etc. It does wonders for the self-esteem. Shaucha also means cleanliness of thoughts, actions, and language. Do you ever notice how you feel when you think nasty thoughts? Are you aware of the repercussions of your dirty deeds? Is it really worth it? Why not save that choice word for the appropriate time that it is meant for, like that, "Damn!" when you stub your toe. Would you drink water out of a dirty glass, or eat food off of a dirty plate? I didn't think so. So why insist on keeping a pure soul in an impure vessel? Maybe it's time for spring cleaning.

2. Santosha: contentment

Stop worrying about the Jones's and what they have. Who cares what color the grass is on the other side? If the glass is half-empty, bottoms up!

3. Tapas: austerity

Why keep something you can't use? Don't be a hoarder, materially, spiritually, or otherwise. Feng Shui your life. Stop carrying dead weight and hanging on to old baggage, it only slows you down. Why continue with a technique in your Sadhana (spiritual practice) that no longer serves a purpose? That's like crossing a river with a canoe to reach a mountain to climb, and carrying the canoe to the summit, instead of leaving it at the riverbank. Please stop burning your brain cells out with useless information. Gain knowledge on what you can use. Like my teacher told me, "The day of the lecture is over. Theory without practice is useless, it's time to do the work."

4. Swadhyaya: introspection

At the entrance to the temple of the Oracle at Delphi is a statement borrowed from the Egyptians that is a primary lesson of all spiritual disciplines: "Know Thyself." Ramana Maharshi has made famous one of the simplest (does not mean easy) ways to 'know thyself.' That is to ask oneself,
"Who am I?"
Try it sometimes, repeatedly ask yourself that one simple question, and the responses you come up with just may surprise you. It helps to have a guide along the journey in order to keep one's ego from attaching to any false image(s) of oneself. In the Zen tradition, any concept or idea that comes to mind should be shunned, but don't make an effort to shun, or you are creating another attachment. In the Taoist tradition, you let go and release what you are not, and all that will be left is the real you. So, who are you?

5. Ishwarapranidhana: devotion to God

A loose, 'literal' translation would be 'every breath is a meditation on/of God.' Ishvara: God. Prana: breath. Dhyana: meditation. This should be a familiar concept for people of all cultures, disciplines, and religions. In the Christian tradition, it's the same idea of being 'saved.' In the Muslim tradition, it's the same as proclaiming that there is no other God but Allah, and Muhammed is His Messenger. In the Jewish tradition, it is following the laws of Moses. In the...you get the picture, the list goes on and on, but the premise is the same: recognizing the creative intelligence of the Universe and dedicating one's life to it in gratitude. Feel free to debate who, what, when, where, why, and how it is, just don't do it with me. I don't have that kind of time to waste. Ishwarapranidhana has already filled my schedule for this lifetime.

III. Asana: Posture

The Asanas, or postures of Hatha Yoga is what the general public thinks of as the totality of Yoga. This is due to a lack of education and what is available the populous at large due to the "Hollywood" style Yoga teachers. Don't get me wrong, I have nothing against this style of practice or its teachers and practitioners, because at least people are getting exercise and an introduction to Yoga. To me, this is like saying a burger, fries, and a soda is a healthy meal. Yes, it will keep you from starving to death, but it needs some more balance. The only thing I'll say about posture that I've been taught is to keep your spine relatively straight throughout your life, so that energy can flow freely. Do you, the reader, remember your parent(s), grandparent(s), or teacher(s) telling you to sit up straight? They were right, and were teaching Asana whether they knew it or not.

IV. Pranayam

Also known as Chi-Gung in Chinese, Pranayam is the process of using the breath to regulate energy. The way one breathes influences mood, health, and general longevity. This happens for several different reasons. Breathing is a process, and the only process of the autonomic nervous system that can be manipulated, and its manipulation influences all other bodily functions, from digestion to your heartbeat. In the Chinese Five Element Theory, there are five Zhang Fu organs (liver, heart, spleen, lungs, and kidneys) that are massaged directly by the diaphragm, or indirectly by the pressure induced by the diaphragm on the organs. In India, there is a Yoga called Swara Yoga, that was taught by Mahaguru Satyananda Saraswati, explaining in detail the importance of the breath as it is breathed in alternate nostrils. In Genesis it is stated that God blew the breath of life into a lump of clay and it became a living being. The importance of the breath cannot be overstated, so please don't waste your breath.

V. Pratyahara: Involution

Pratyhara, or involution, is the process of shutting out external stimuli via the sense organs, and paying attention to the sights and sounds on the inside. This also applies to tastes and smells, and especially the way one feels. The way one feels may even be considered the primary stimulus for all other senses, internal or external. Light 'touches' receptors in the eye, sending signals to the brain as sight. Sound waves impact the eardrum, thereby imparting the sensation of sound, et cetera, et cetera. The way you feel on the inside, also known as your emotions, influences your perception of the internal world. Yet Pratyahara is beyond mere emotion, especially in the state of meditation, when different sights and sounds will be experienced. To be discerned are the mental projections of psychic garbage being disposed of by the nervous system in a state of repose, from deeper levels of insight expressing themselves from the core of one's being. Listen for the sound of silence, and one day, you just might hear it.

VI. Dharana: Concentration

Once all external distractions have been subverted, one can have single-minded concentration, also known as Dharana. I'm pretty sure when most people hear the word 'meditation,' that an image of a person in a long robe sitting cross-legged staring at a candle comes to mind. This is not meditation, but a tool to facilitate meditation. Dharana, single- minded concentration, is the goal aspired for, and a pre-requisite for meditation. Only when the mind has attained this focus, can the mind drop everything. Think about it, it's easier to turn off the television when nothing else is on, than to turn everything off in your home at once (unless you have a Clapper). When this single-minded concentration dissolves into concentrating on absolutely nothing at all, meditation has just begun.

VII. Dhyana: Meditation

"When I sit real still, close my eyes, and be quiet, I can listen to God."
-Lily, age 8

VIII. Samadhi: Bliss

Samadhi, or bliss, is not necessarily a practice or discipline, but rather an after-effect of the spiritual path of Yoga. It is the cigarette after a large meal, the drunkness of drinking, the high after smoking a joint, or the orgasm of sex, only with much longer lasting affects. Samadhi is something that usually occurs when the seeker stops looking for it as an expectation. The harder you try, the more elusive Samadhi becomes, yet only through consistent effort may it be experienced. Haven't you heard the statement, "Let go and let God?" This should be used in conjunction with, "Take one step towards God, and God takes two steps towards you." So, what is Samadhi and how does it feel? Walk your spiritual path with perseverance and sincerity, and the answer will reveal itself. I won't spoil your experience. Enjoy your yogurt.

3. A Taste of Tantra

My teacher/guru/brother/friend, Sunyata Saraswati, has been
teaching Tantra for over fifty years. During our time living
together, I had often shared with him some of my poetry. He
would look over the rim of his glasses and tell me,
 "Scotty, you need to publish these, man."
So, many years overdue, but right on time, I am sharing with
you some of my poetry, inspired by my Tantric practice.

sunrise:

if i was yours
every morning
that God gives We
my lips would awaken U
gently placing a smile
on your cheek
the one closest to me

dreaming of an oasis:

said i had to go
then let go of your hands
now i'm alone
and crossing burning sands
i know nothing
except
the sound of your grace
the warmth of your embrace
the silence
and coldness
of space
when nobody's there
and no one cares
i don't know where U are
tears i can't control
water my lonely soul
one way to go
trying to find home.

labor pains:

as I am birthed
from your Cosmic Womb
my first and only desire
is for your heavenly embrace
the cause of my suffering
is the illusion
of my separation from U
when I am weaned
from your breasts
i am liberated
my strongest attachment
dissolves
as I realize
everything I grasp for
i must let go
in order to grow
until my aspirations
expire
into Union with the Absolute
when it's time
to be reunited
with U.

discernment:

if ever
i questioned
what Love is
U answered it for me
with crystal clear
clarity
accepting who I am
though I may be
still searching
for the answer.

human being:

when
i
stopped
trying
to
do
every
thing
i
became
a
human
Being.

The Lord's Prayer

Our Mother
Which art in Heaven
Hallowed be Thy Name
Thy Kingdom Come
Thy Will be Done
On Earth
as it is in Heaven
Give us this day
Our daily bread
Forgive us our trespasses
as we forgive those
Who trespass against us
Lead us not into temptation
and deliver us from evil
For thine is the Kingdom
the Power
and the Glory
Forever
Amen.

I love my best friend, Latoya. My phone just received a text message, and guess who it is? Latoya. She doesn't know I am writing this, and this is the message sent to me, as I was writing, "I love my best friend, Latoya.":

Smile,
life
to live.
Express,
Feel stress.
Discover beauty,
Enjoy like, and feel love.
Love you too Scotty

Wow! Twenty years, six children, and three marriages (not with each other) between the two of us, the love has not changed. The sexual attraction is there, minus sexual tension. An uncanny understanding exists, and also a sometimes brutal honesty. I am Shiva, and she is my Kali-Ma. My ego lies beneath her dancing feet, the heads of my false personalities are severed and strewn as jewelry around her neck, and I am in bliss. Every time I am around her, a great deal of sexual energy arises, along with a sense of clarity and acceptance. Our hearts are content with simply being in each others'
presence. No lust exists towards each other, and we feel orgasmic without touching or even saying a word. Our bodies have never been in sexual union, yet our existence is eternally bound in a loving embrace. It is an intimate spiritual experience.
It is a taste of Tantra.

sincerely being

Anahata opening
realizing she loves me
just because i am
she tells me
she is me
loving the man in me
says she
i'm in love with myself
sincerely being
whom I'm supposed to be
blessed by divinity
from antiquity to eternity
an answer to my prayers
as I kneel to humble myself
and the evening sun sets
my head kisses the ground
in gratitude for U
loving me.

4. Immortality

Fifteen minutes of fame. Do you know what that fifteen minutes of fame is? Your eulogy. No matter life's accomplishments, we are all going to die.

Immortality:

Love is Life
Death is Freedom
there is no
in between
to grant one Freedom
is the highest level of Love
that's what
Life is
Love
those here before
those here now
and those yet to come
for all have two things
in common
Life and Death
and Death loves Life enough
to let it be Free.

5. The Zen Mind

About the author:

Scotty:
He was a first child
taking part of his father's name
he chose his own future
tempered by his own choices.
Searching for meaning to his life
he continues his sojourn
until he finds his reflection
in the mirror of time.
-by Darryl T. Fisher, Sr. (my uncle)